Read what our customers have to say...

"*Let me say that it is a great piece of software indeed. SAS Learning Edition is so intuitive, well organized, and well documented that students can start producing professional-level statistics and charts in almost no time. I enjoy using your software and will be glad to recommend SAS Learning Edition to anybody who has need for high-quality statistical processing.*"

Zoran Cvijanovic
Visiting Instructor of Computer Science
Colgate University

"*After working with the SAS Learning Edition and SAS Self-Paced e-Learning products—and without any prior experience with the material—I was able to interview for and secure a position as a SAS Data Analyst. The training proved to be very valuable in providing a thorough and interesting foundation in SAS programming. SAS Learning Edition and SAS Self-Paced e-Learning are wonderful training tools and I give them my wholehearted endorsement.*"

John Spinelli

"*SAS Learning Edition is very user friendly, and it provides a self-learning environment for the new student/user with a point-and-click option which automatically generates SAS code. On the other hand more advanced users can go directly into the enhanced editor and write code. That possibility allows for the teaching of SAS software to those students that will use the full-blown version later in their careers.*"

Zoran Bursac, Ph.D., M.P.H.
Assistant Professor
University of Arkansas for Medical Sciences
College of Public Health / College of Medicine

Join the SAS® Learning Edition community!

Become part of the growing community of SAS learners. The SAS Learning Edition Web site has links to resources that will help you get the most from SAS Learning Edition. You will find links to resources for learning more about SAS, including SAS Self-Paced e-Learning, SAS OnlineDoc®, and Books by Users Press.

support.sas.com/le

SAS® Learning Edition 2.0

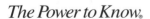

The Power to Know.

The correct bibliographic citation for this manual is as follows: SAS Institute Inc. 2004. *SAS® Learning Edition 2.0*. Cary, NC: SAS Institute Inc.

SAS® Learning Edition 2.0

Copyright © 2004, SAS Institute Inc., Cary, NC, USA

ISBN 1-59047-460-0

SAS Institute Inc., SAS Campus Drive, Cary, North Carolina 27513.

1st printing, July 2004
2nd printing, February 2005

SAS Publishing provides a complete selection of books and electronic products to help customers use SAS software to its fullest potential. For more information about our e-books, e-learning products, CDs, and hard-copy books, visit the SAS Publishing Web site at **support.sas.com/pubs** or call 1-800-727-3228.

Contents

Chapter 7 Summarizing Data and Creating Reports

Chapter 1

IN THIS CHAPTER

What is SAS Learning Edition?

Introducing SAS Learning Edition

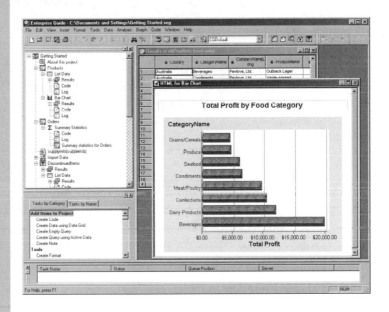

What is SAS Learning Edition?

SAS Learning Edition combines SAS software with SAS Enterprise Guide, a point-and-click environment that provides access to much of the functionality of SAS. You can use SAS Learning Edition to access, manipulate, analyze, and create reports on your own data as well as on the sample data that is included with the software.

In SAS Learning Edition, SAS software and SAS Enterprise Guide work together. SAS Enterprise Guide uses the execution power of the server to access data and run SAS processes. As you do your work in SAS Enterprise Guide, you are generating SAS code behind the scenes. When you finish a task, this code is sent to SAS for processing and the results are returned to SAS Enterprise Guide.

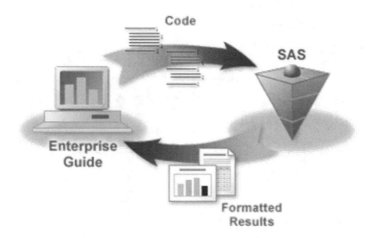

When you started SAS Learning Edition, you may have noticed that SAS Enterprise Guide opened. You can use all the features of SAS Enterprise Guide without knowing how to program in SAS. If SAS programming is what you want to do, you can use the Code Editor in SAS Enterprise Guide to write, edit, and submit SAS programs.

SAS Enterprise Guide can access SAS that is installed on a local or remote server in several different operating environments. For SAS Learning Edition, SAS and SAS Enterprise Guide are both installed on your local PC, and SAS Enterprise Guide accesses the local copy of SAS.

If you have used SAS before...

If you are already a SAS user, you may be more familiar with the SAS Display Manager System (DMS), which includes the SAS Explorer, Enhanced Editor, Log, and Output windows. Although you can access SAS and use these windows if you prefer, there are some tools, such as VIEWTABLE, that are not included in SAS Learning Edition.

The topics in this book teach you how to use the point-and-click features of SAS Enterprise Guide to perform tasks that you may have done in the past by writing SAS programs. Using SAS Enterprise Guide, you can write, edit, and submit SAS programs. You can even edit the code that is generated from a point-and-click task. If you are interested in using SAS Learning Edition to learn programming, you can find a complete library of SAS programming lessons on the SAS Self-Paced e-Learning Web site at `http://www.sas.com/apps/elearning/elearning_category_welcome.jsp`. You can use either the SAS Enterprise Guide interface or the SAS DMS interface to complete these lessons. The Web site also has lessons specifically for SAS Enterprise Guide.

SAS Learning Edition includes Base SAS and limited versions of the following SAS software components:
- SAS/GRAPH
- SAS/STAT
- SAS/QC
- SAS/ETS.

Because Graph Maps and MDDB Server are not included in SAS Learning Edition, you will not be able to work with MDDBs or run Graph Map Chart tasks in SAS Enterprise Guide.

 You have finished **What is SAS Learning Edition?** In the next section, you open SAS Enterprise Guide and create a new project.

Getting Started

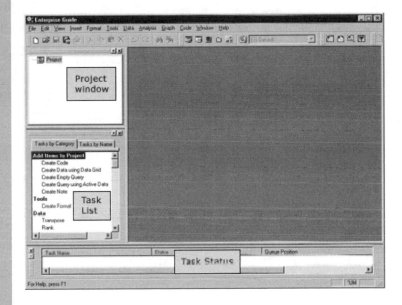

Starting up

SAS Enterprise Guide uses projects to manage a collection of related data, tasks, code, and results. Only one project can be open at any one time in SAS Enterprise Guide.

Open SAS Enterprise Guide

Double-click the SAS Enterprise Guide icon on your desktop or select **Enterprise Guide** from the Start menu.

Create a new project

Each time you start SAS Enterprise Guide, you must either create a new project or select an existing project to open. In this task, you create a new project to store the data and results that you create as you work through this book.

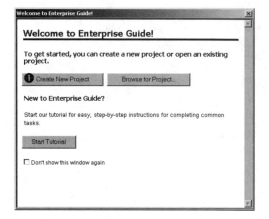

❶ In the Welcome to Enterprise Guide! window, click **Create New Project**.

❷ The new project is created and you are ready to begin the tasks in this book.

    To open a project that you have saved in the past, click **Browse for Project**, navigate to the correct location, and then double-click the project name. ∎

Touring SAS Enterprise Guide

Take a look around

When you start SAS Enterprise Guide for the first time, you see the default workspace layout. The default workspace consists of windows (Project, Task List, Task Status), menus, toolbars, and the agent.

Additional windows, such as the Server List window, are available from the View menu.

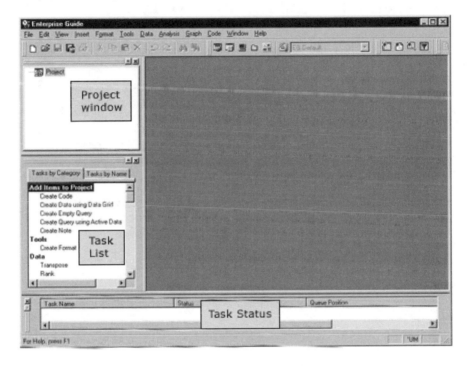

To learn more about customizing the toolbars and other features of SAS Enterprise Guide, select Help ➜ Enterprise Guide Help and browse through the topics under Customizing Enterprise Guide. ■

About the Project window

SAS Enterprise Guide uses projects to manage a collection of related data, tasks, code, and results. Only one project can be open at a time in SAS Enterprise Guide. The Project window displays the active project and its associated data, code, notes, and results.

If you close the Project window and want to restore it, click the Project tool (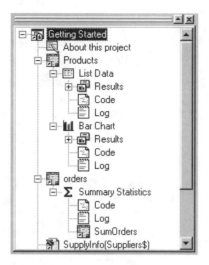) on the toolbar or select View ➜ Project.

About the Task List

You use the Task List to select the tasks that you want to run on your data. To begin a task, first you select the data that you want to analyze, and then you double-click the task in the Task List.

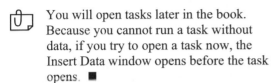 You will open tasks later in the book. Because you cannot run a task without data, if you try to open a task now, the Insert Data window opens before the task opens. ■

The **Tasks by Category** tab lists individual tasks, grouped by type. The **Tasks by Name** tab lists individual tasks alphabetically. This tab also lists the SAS procedure that is related to the task.

If you close the task window and want to restore it, click the Task List tool (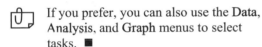) on the toolbar, or select **View ➜ Task List**.

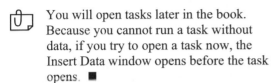 If you prefer, you can also use the **Data**, **Analysis**, and **Graph** menus to select tasks. ■

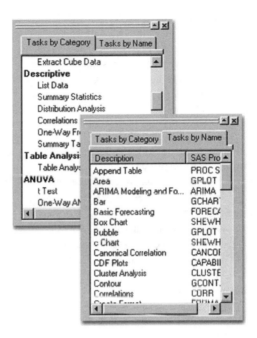

Accessing the help

Help is available for all tasks in SAS Enterprise Guide. The help includes a table of contents, an index, and a search feature. You can also bookmark favorite help topics for quick reference. There are several ways to access help in SAS Enterprise Guide.

- Help menu
  Select **Help ➜ Enterprise Guide Help** to open the main SAS Enterprise Guide help.

- Help buttons and F1
  All task windows and many of the other tools windows have context-sensitive Help buttons. When you click the Help button in a task window, the help for that task opens. You can also press F1 to open help for the active window.

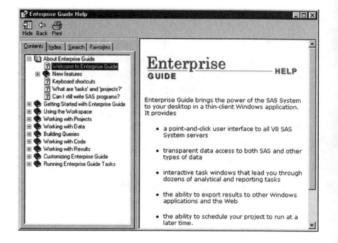

You can find the help topic that you want by using the tabs on the left side of the SAS Enterprise Guide Help window. The tabs contain the following information:

- Contents – SAS Enterprise Guide help topics, organized by task and subject. Double-click the book icons to display SAS Enterprise Guide help topics.
- Index – SAS Enterprise Guide and SAS programming help topics in alphabetical order.
- Search – an interface for entering search terms.
- Favorites – a list of help topics that you bookmark for quick reference.

 You have finished **Touring SAS Enterprise Guide**. In the next section, you learn about what you will be doing in this book.

Previewing what you will learn

Learn to create basic reports

In the first part of this step-by-step book, you learn to do the basic tasks that you will perform each time you create a report in SAS Enterprise Guide:

- create or open a project
- add data to a project or select the data that you want to use
- run tasks to analyze and report on the data that you have selected.

After adding sample data to your project, you run tasks to create a listing report and a bar chart. You also learn to customize report styles and use the graph controls.

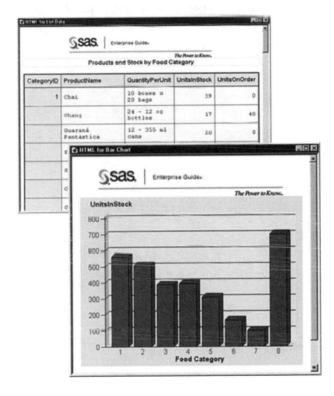

Learn to modify data for reports

After you have learned to create basic reports, you learn to modify data for reports. The information that you want in a report is not always available from one data file. In this section, you modify data by using queries and other tasks, and then create reports from the modified data. You will do the following:

- filter data by using a query, and then create a listing report
- join data and change column properties in a query, and then create a frequency count and a listing report
- create summary data and add it to an existing query, and then create a bar chart and a summary table.

After finishing this book, you will have learned to use the primary features of SAS Enterprise Guide, and you will be ready to start working on your own.

 You have finished **Previewing what you will learn.** In the next section, you learn to do a few more tasks in the Project window.

Adding Data to a Project

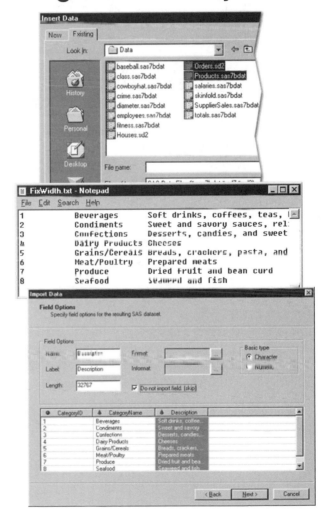

Setting up the project

From the Project window, you can manage all of your work in SAS Enterprise Guide. After you have added data to your project, you can run tasks that perform analyses and generate reports, and everything will be stored in the project. You can edit, rename, delete, and rearrange items in the Project window. You can also save an entire project for later use.

In this section, you create a note for the project and save the project.

Create a note for the project

You can create notes to accompany tables, results, or the project. In this example, you create a note to accompany your project.

❶ Make sure that the project is selected in the Project window, and select Insert ➡ Note.

❷ In the **Name** box, type About this project. Click **OK**.

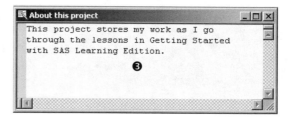

❸ In the note window, type a message to accompany the project.

❹ Close the note window. The note text is automatically saved. You can reopen the note by double-clicking the note icon in the Project window.

Save the project

You can save your project and its contents. Projects can be saved to any location, including a location on another server.

❶ Select File ➡ Save Project As.

❷ In the Save As window, type `Getting Started.seg` in the File name box.

❸ Select a new location for the project or keep the default location. Click Save.

 Project files are saved with a .seg extension. ■

 You have finished Setting up the project. In the next section, you add data to the project.

Adding data to the project

About data in SAS Enterprise Guide

Before you can create reports or run analyses, you must add data to your project. Using SAS Enterprise Guide, you can access the following:

- local or remote SAS data sets
- files from databases such as Oracle and DB2 that have licensed SAS database engines
- local data in other formats (such as Microsoft Excel, Microsoft Access, Lotus, text, HTML, ODBC, and OLE/DB)
- MDDBs with additional SAS software.

SAS Enterprise Guide requires all data that it accesses to be in table format. A table is made up of a set of rows (observations) and columns (variables). Columns contain either character or numeric data values.

The tasks in this book use data in the SAS Enterprise Guide sample data folder.

Add SAS Data

In this task, you add two SAS data sets to
your project.

❶   Select Insert ➡ Data.
❷   In the Insert Data window, click the
     Existing tab. The first time you insert
     data, the location opens to your
     Personal folder.

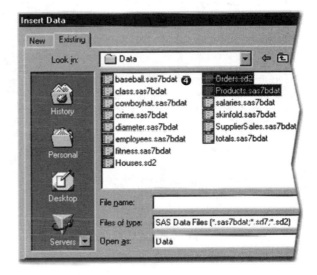

> If the window does not open to
> your Personal folder, click the
> Personal folder icon on the left
> side of the window. ■

❸   Double-click Enterprise Guide
     Sample, and then double-click **Data**.

❹   By default, SAS Data Files is selected
     as the file type. Select **Orders.sd2**.
     Then press and hold the CTRL key
     and select **Products.sas7bdat**.

❺   Click OK. The two tables are added to
     the project, and each one opens in a
     data grid.

> When you insert data into a
> project, you are creating a
> reference to the data. SAS
> Enterprise Guide does not make a
> new copy of the file. ■

❻   To keep your workspace uncluttered,
     close both data grids. You can reopen
     a table by double-clicking its icon in
     the Project window.

> To change the order of items in
> your project, click the item that
> you want to move and drag it up or
> down the project tree. ■

Add other data types

SAS Enterprise Guide gives you transparent access to data that is created by SAS and other vendors' software. In this task, you add a Microsoft Excel file to your project.

❶ Select Insert ➤ Data. The sample data directory opens automatically.

❷ In the Files of type drop-down list, select Microsoft Excel Files(*.xls).

❸ Double-click SupplyInfo.xls to open the Excel Workbook.

❹ Double-click Suppliers$. The Suppliers$ worksheet opens in the data grid, and the table is added to the project.

❺ Close the Suppliers$ data grid.

    To delete any item from the Project window, right-click the item and select Delete from the shortcut menu. The reference to the item is deleted from the project. The item itself is not deleted. ∎

    You have finished Adding data to the project. In the next section, you use the Import Data task to create a SAS data set from a text file.

Importing data from a text file

The Import Data task enables you to create SAS data sets from Microsoft Excel files and from delimited and fixed-width text files. In this section, you use the Import Data task to create a SAS data set from a text file that contains category identification numbers and names.

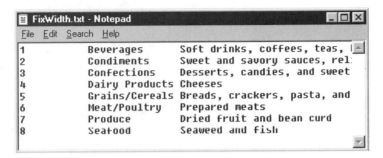

After the data is imported and saved as a SAS data set, you can join it to the Products data set so that a descriptive category name is available for food categories.

Select the text file

In this task, you select the data type and the text file that you want to import.

❶ Select Tools ➜ Import Data. The Import Data task opens.

❷ On the Data Type page, make sure that Text Files is selected. Click Next.

❸ On the Data Source page, open the SAS Enterprise Guide Sample Data folder. Select FixWidth.txt.

❹ Click Next.

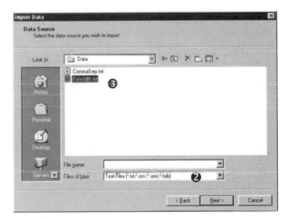

Select the text format and field widths

In this task, you accept the default selections for text format and field widths.

❶ On the Text Format page, make sure that Fixed Width is selected.

❷ Click Next. On the Field Widths (Column Breaks) page, the field widths have been entered correctly.

❸ Click Next.

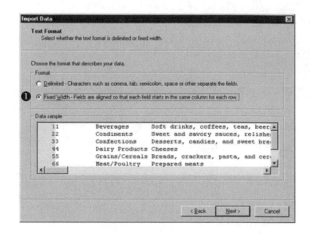

Set field options

In this task, you eliminate the Description field from the import process.

❶ On the First Row Columns page, you can accept the default setting because the first row of the text file does not contain column headings. Click Next.

❷ On the Field Characteristics page, click Next.

❸ On the Field Options page, click the heading for the Description column and select the **Do not import field** check box.

❹ Click Next.

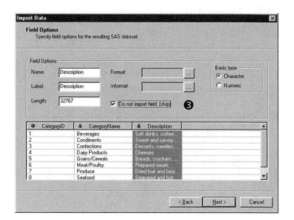

Import the file and rename it

In this task, you select a location to save the data and then import it. Then you rename the data in the Project window.

❶ On the Save page, accept the default SASUSER location. In the File name box, type `categories`. The data is saved as a SAS data set.

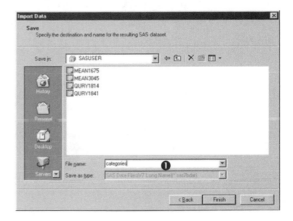

📑 You will see a different Save page if you checked Use DATA step if possible on the Data Type page, or if you are running without SAS installed locally. In those cases, the data that you are importing and the output data must be saved on the same server, so the Save page shows valid locations on that server.

❷ Click Finish. The data opens in the data grid.

❸ Close the data grid.

ℹ️ To see the properties of a table in your project, right-click the table in the Project window and select Properties from the shortcut menu.

___

✅ You have finished Importing data from a text file. In the next section, you create a simple listing report.

Chapter 4

Running Tasks and Modifying Output

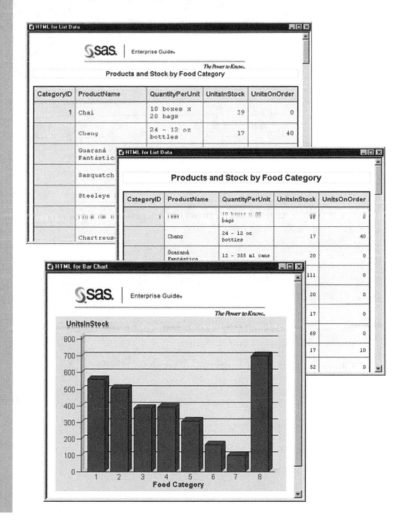

Creating and modifying a listing report

The simple listing report that you generate in this section introduces you to using task windows in SAS Enterprise Guide. Once you are familiar with using task windows, you can perform any appropriate task on your data.

Let's suppose that you want a report that lists products, food category, amount of stock on hand, and amount of stock on order. In this section, you use the List Data task to create a report with this information. Then you modify the task to group the product list by food category. At the end of this section, you will have a report that looks like the report below.

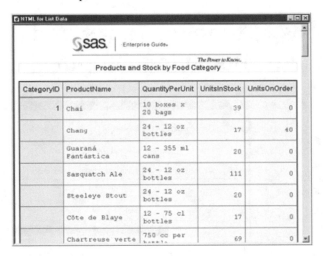

Select the data and start the List Data task

Before you begin a task, the data that you want to work with must be active in the project. This task uses the Products table.

❶ In the Project window, click the Products table to make it the active data.

❷ Click the **Tasks by Category** tab and scroll down the list to the Descriptive category.

❸ Double-click the **List Data** task. The task window opens.

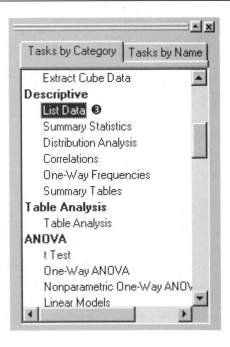

Assign variables to roles

In all SAS Enterprise Guide tasks, you must designate the variables that you want to analyze and assign them to roles. For the List Data task, you designate which variables to print and the order in which you want them to appear in the output.

❶ On the Columns tab, press the CTRL key and select the following variables in the **Variables to assign** list:

- ProductName
- CategoryID
- QuantityPerUnit
- UnitsInStock
- UnitsOnOrder.

Drag the selected variables to the List variables role.

📝 To display the properties of the variables in the **Variables to assign** list, right-click a variable and select **Properties.** ∎

❷ Select CategoryID under the List **variables** role and move it to the top of the list by dragging it up. This changes the order of the variables so that CategoryID is printed in the first column of the results.

ℹ You can also change the variable order by selecting the variable that you want to move and clicking the up and down arrow buttons below the List data roles box.

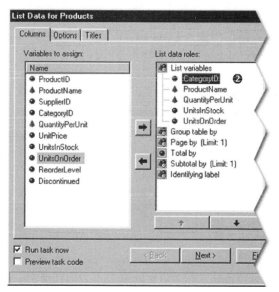

Set options

Most SAS Enterprise Guide tasks have one or
more tabs with additional options that you can
set for the task. Options are grouped on tabs by
their function. The most commonly used options
are set by default.

❶ Click the Options tab. Notice that some
options are already selected by default.

❷ Clear the Print the row number check box.

To move through the tabs in a task
window, click the Next and Back buttons
or click the tab that you want to open. ■

As you select options in the task window,
SAS Enterprise Guide generates the SAS
code that creates the results. If you want
to see the code, select the Preview task
code check box.

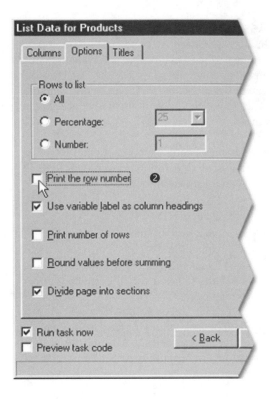

View the results

In this task, you view the results of the List Data
task.

❶ Click **Finish** to run the task. The results of
the List Data task open automatically.

❷ Scroll through the results. The report
contains the variables that you assigned in
the order that you specified.

❸ Close the HTML for List Data window.

ℹ️ To save your work without running the
task, clear the **Run task now** check box.
Then click **Finish**. Your task information
is saved, and you can reopen the task by
double-clicking the task item in the
Project window.

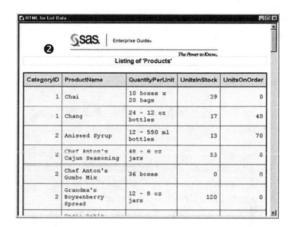

Modify the task

After you have finished a task, it is saved in the project tree and you can open the task and modify it. In this task, you modify the List Data task to group the results by the CategoryID variable.

❶ In the Project window, double-click the List Data icon that was added under the Products table.

❷ In the List Data for Products window, click the **Columns** tab. Drag **CategoryID** to the **Group table by** role. This moves the CategoryID variable from one role to another. Notice that the default sort order is ascending order.

❸ In the **Variables to assign** list, click **CategoryID** and drag it to the **Identifying label** role. The CategoryID variable is now assigned to two roles. By assigning this variable to the **Identifying label** role, the values of CategoryID appear only in the first row of the group of data that is associated with a CategoryID value.

❹ Click the **Titles** tab. In the **Section** box, select **Report Titles**.

❺ In the **Text** box, delete the default title and type `Products and Stock by Food Category`.

❻ In the **Section** box, select **List Data Footnotes**. Delete the default footnote.

View the new results

In this task, you view the changes that you made
to the report.

❶ Click **Finish**. In the confirmation window,
click **Yes** so that the results of this task
overwrite the previous results. If you click
No, the task is saved as a separate item in
the project.

❷ Scroll through the results. Notice that
products are grouped by CategoryID and
that the CategoryID value appears only in
the first row for that group. The title that you
specified appears at the top of the report,
and there is no footnote at the bottom.

❸ Close the HTML for List Data window.

❗ To view the results in an external
browser, right-click the HTML item in
the Project window and select **Open with**
default browser (*default browser* is the
browser that you have chosen as the
default for your machine).

✅ You have finished **Creating and
modifying a listing report**. In the next
section, you create a bar chart.

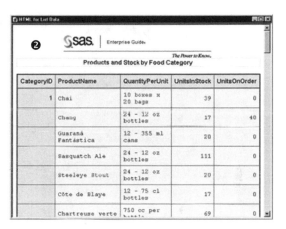

Creating a bar chart and exploring graph controls

Bar charts are used to compare numeric values or statistics among different values of a chart variable. In this section, you create a bar chart that shows the total amount of stock for each food category. Then you learn to use the interactive graph controls to modify elements of the chart.

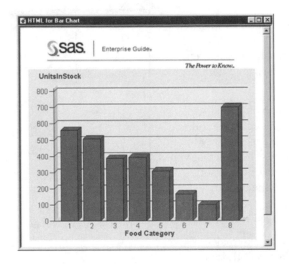

Start the task and select a chart type

In this task, you start the Bar Chart task and select the type of chart that you want to create.

❶ In the Project window, select **Products** to make it the active data set.

❷ On the Enterprise Guide menu bar, select **Graph ➡ Bar**.

You can also open the Bar Chart task window by double-clicking **Bar** in the Task List. ∎

❸ On the **Chart Gallery** tab, double-click the Simple Vertical Bar icon.

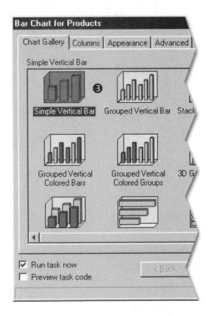

Assign variables to roles

In this task, you first select a column to
chart and then a sum column that
determines the lengths of the bars.

❶ On the Columns tab, drag CategoryID
to the Column to chart role.

❷ Drag UnitsInStock to the Sum by role.

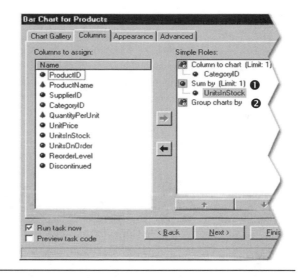

Change a column label

You can change the editable column
properties in the data grid or in a task
window. In this task, you change the label
of the CategoryID column.

❶ On the Columns tab, right-click the
CategoryID column and select
Properties from the shortcut menu.
You can right-click the column in
either pane of the window.

❷ In the CategoryID Properties window,
type Food Category in the Label
box.

❸ Click OK.

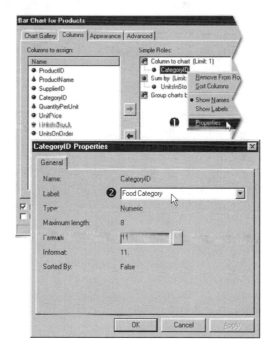

Create and view the chart

After you have set the options that you
want for the graph, you are ready to run
the task. In this task, you generate and
view the bar chart.

❶ Click **Finish** to create the graph.

❷ Take a look at the graph. Notice
that the label that you typed for
CategoryID is used as the label for the
x-axis. There is no default title text for
graphs, so you must specify a title on
the **Appearance** tab if you want one.

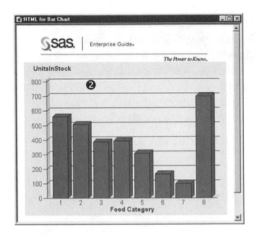

Change the bar and data options

If you are using ActiveX or Java output for
graphics, you can change many graphics
options interactively. In this task, you
explore a few of the interactive graph
options. Any changes that you make in this
way are not saved.

❶ Right-click a bar in the graph and
select **Bar Options**.

❷ In the Bar Options window, select the
Show labels check box. Notice that
data values appear at the top of each
bar. Click **OK**.

❸ Right-click the graph and select
Options ➡ Data.

❹ In the Data Options window, click the
Statistic drop-down box and select
Percentage. Click **Apply**. Notice that
the chart now shows the percentage
that each food category represents.
Click **OK**.

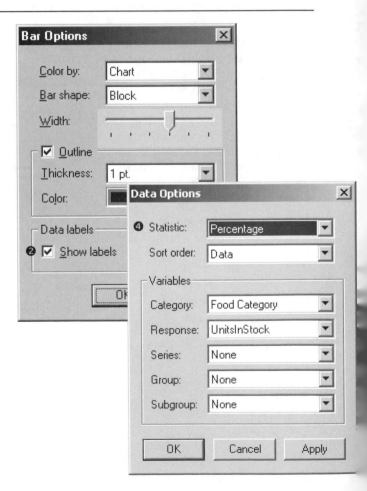

Change the graph type

In this task, you change the graph type to a
pie chart.

❶ Right-click the graph and select **Chart
Type ➜ Pie**. The chart changes to a
pie chart.

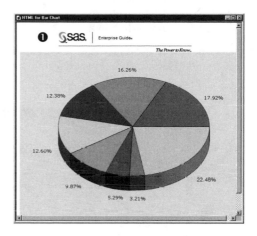

🗒️   To save an image of the graph that
you have created with the graph
control, right-click the graph and
select **Save As**. The graph that you
save in this way is not interactive.
■

❷ Close the HTML for Bar Chart
window. The changes that you made
to the chart are not saved. Permanent
changes to the graph can be made by
reopening the task window and
selecting new options.

✔️   You have finished **Creating a bar
chart and exploring graph controls**.
In the next section, you create a
new report style and explore
additional results options.

Customizing report styles

Results of the tasks that you run in SAS Enterprise Guide are generated in HTML format with a cascading style sheet (CSS) applied. You can use any of the predefined styles for your results, or you can create your own style by using the Style Editor.

In this section, you create a new style, save it, and apply it to your results. The style that you create is similar to the EG Default style, but it does not use the banner image.

Create and save a new style

By default, results have the EG Default style applied. You can change the style to one of the other styles that are included with SAS Enterprise Guide, or you can define your own style by using the Style Editor. In this task, you create and save a new style. Then you set the new style as the default style for results.

❶ Select **Tools ➡ Style Manager**. In the Style Manager window, the EGDefault style is selected. Click Edit.

❷ In the Edit Style window, click the Images tab. Clear the Use banner image check box.

❸ Click Save As. In the Save Style window, type `Company Style`.

❹ Click **OK** to close the Save Style window, then click **OK** to close the Edit Style window.

❺ In the Style Manager window, select Company Style. Click **Set as Default**. This style will be applied to the results that you generate from this point forward.

❻ Click **OK** to close the Style Manager window.

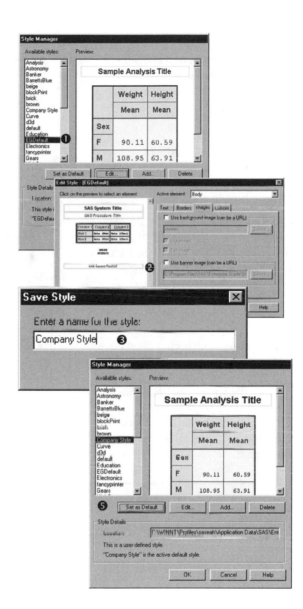

Apply the new style

You can open existing output and apply
any style that is available in SAS
Enterprise Guide. In this task, you apply
the Company Style style sheet to your
listing report.

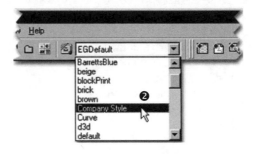

❶ In the Project window, double-click
the HTML results under the List Data
item. The results open with the
EGDefault style applied.

❷ On the main toolbar, select **Company
Style** from the style drop-down list.
The new style is applied to the List
Data results.

❸ Close the HTML for List Data
window.

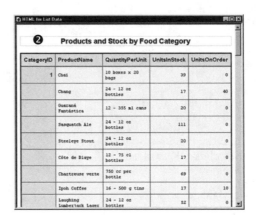

ⓘ In addition to changing the style
that is applied to HTML results,
you can also select various output
formats such as PDF, RTF, and
text output. To change the output
type, select **Tools Options** and
click the **Results** tab in the Options
window.

✔ You have finished **Customizing
report styles**. In the next section,
you use the Query Builder to filter
data.

Filtering Data and Creating a Report

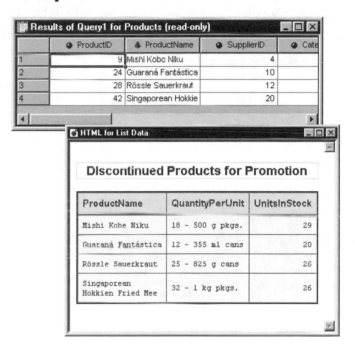

Filtering data

The Query Builder enables you to extract data from one or more tables according to criteria that you specify. When you filter data, the query extracts only the rows that meet the condition that you set in the filter. Filter conditions are based on values of columns in the data or columns that are calculated from the data.

In this section, you prepare the data so that you can create a list of discontinued items that the company will sell in a special Internet promotion. For this report, you want only the rows in the Products table where the following conditions are true:

- the value of Discontinued is 1
  and
- the value of UnitsInStock is greater than 0.

Both conditions must be true in order for the row to be included in the query results.

Select data and start the Query Builder

You can open a query with or without data. In this task, you select the Products table and then begin the query.

❶ In the Project window, select **Products** to make it active.

❷ Select **Tools ➡ Query ➡ Create from Active Data**. The Query Builder opens.

❸ In the Query Builder, the data and variables are listed on the left side of the window. You use this list to select columns to filter and include in the output data.

ⓘ Behind the scenes, the Query Builder generates SQL code. To view this code, select **Show preview of the generated code**.

Set the first filter

In this task, you set the filter for discontinued items. The data values in the Discontinued column are 1 (discontinued) and 0 (available). You want to include only rows in which the value of Discontinued is equal to 1.

❶ In the Query Builder, make sure that the Filter Data tab is selected.

❷ Drag the Discontinued column to the filter area on the right. The Edit Filter Condition window opens.

❸ In the Value box, type 1.

To see a list of all the values for a column, click Column Values in the Filter constants area. ■

❹ Click OK. The filter is represented in the filter area.

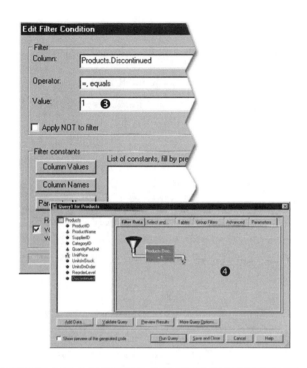

Set the second filter

In this task, you set the filter for items that are in stock. You want to include only rows in which the value of UnitsInStock is greater than 0.

❶ Drag UnitsInStock to the end of the first filter, and drop it when the cursor displays AND. The Edit Filter Condition window opens.

❷ From the Operator drop-down list, select >, greater than.

❸ In the Value box, type 0.

❹ Click OK. The filter is represented in the filter area.

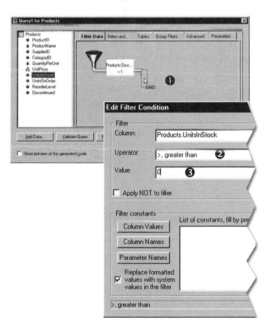

View the data

In this task, you view the results of your query.

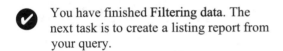

❶ In the Query Builder, click **Run Query**.

❷ The list of discontinued items opens in the data grid. Notice that there are four products that met both filter conditions. The filter does not affect the number of columns that are returned. By default, all columns are included in the query.

❸ In the Project window, right-click **Query1 for Products** and select **Rename**. Type `DiscontinuedItems`.

❹ Close the data grid.

✓ You have finished **Filtering data**. The next task is to create a listing report from your query.

Creating a listing report from filtered data

Now that you have filtered the Products data and created query results that include only the discontinued items in stock, you can use the List Data task to make a formatted report of these items.

The report should list the following:

- product name (ProductName)
- number of items per unit (QuantityPerUnit)
- number of units in stock (UnitsInStock).

When you finish this section, your report will be similar to the one below.

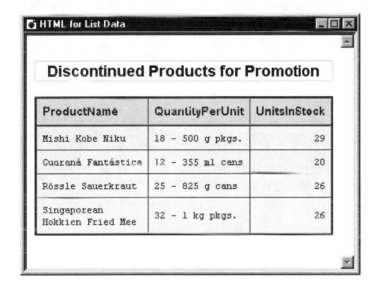

Start the task and assign variables to roles

Just as you can run tasks against data, you can also run tasks against a query. In this task, you use the List Data task with the DiscontinuedItems query.

❶ In the Project window, make sure that **DiscontinuedItems** is selected.

❷ Scroll through the Tasks by Category list to the Descriptive category. Double-click **List Data**. The task window opens.

❸ In the **Variables to assign** box, press the CTRL key and select **ProductName**, **QuantityPerUnit**, and **UnitsInStock**. Drag them to the **List variables** role.

ⓘ You can assign variables to roles by dragging and dropping them or by using the assignment arrows. To use the arrows, select a variable, click ➡️, and select from the list of roles.

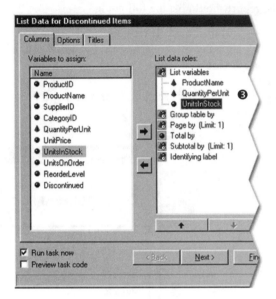

Set options and add a title

In this task, you set options and add a title for the report.

❶ Click the Options tab.

❷ Clear the **Print the row number** check box.

❸ Click the Titles tab.

❹ In the Section box, select **Report Titles**. In the **Text** box, delete the default title and type `Discontinued Products for Promotion`.

❺ In the Section box, select **List Data Footnotes**. In the Text box, delete the default footnote.

View the results

In this task, you view your final report of discontinued items.

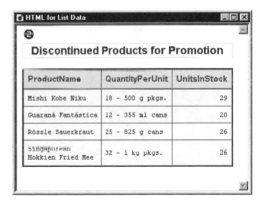

❶ Click Finish.

❷ Notice that the report contains the columns that you specified. The results are formatted using the Company Style style sheet that you created earlier in the book.

❸ Close the HTML for List Data window.

 You have finished **Creating a listing report from filtered data**. In the next section, you join data and create reports.

Joining Data and Creating Reports

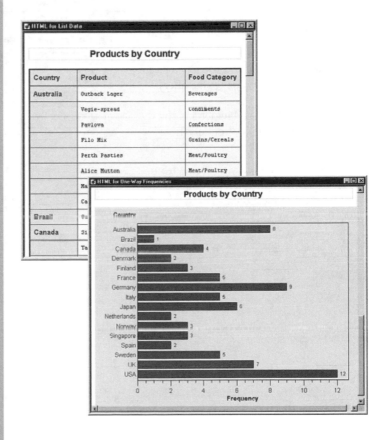

Joining data by using a query

The Query Builder enables you to join data from up to 32 different tables. In this section, you use the Query Builder to join the following tables:

- Products — a SAS data set that contains product information such as name, price, and quantity of stock. It also contains supplier and category identification numbers.
- Suppliers$ — a Microsoft Excel spreadsheet that contains supplier information such as name, address, and country.
- Categories — the new SAS data set that you imported from a text file that contains descriptive information about food categories.

After the query is complete, the data will include information about suppliers. Then you can use the query to create a frequency count and a list of products by country.

Select the data and start the query

In this task, you select the Products data to make it active, and then begin the query.

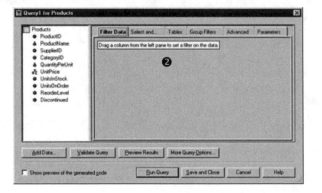

❶ Select the Products data icon in the project tree to make Products the active data set.

❷ Select Tools ➜ Query ➜ Create from Active Data. The Query Builder opens with the Products data.

Join the Suppliers$ table

In this task, you join the Suppliers$ table to the Products table. Both tables have a SupplierID column, so the Query Builder automatically performs the join.

❶ In the Query Builder, click **Add Data**.

❷ In the Add Data window, click the **Project** tab to see a list of the data that has been added to the project. Double-click **SupplyInfo(Suppliers$)** to add it to the query.

❸ In the Query Builder, click the **Tables** tab. Notice that the tables have been automatically joined on the SupplierID column.

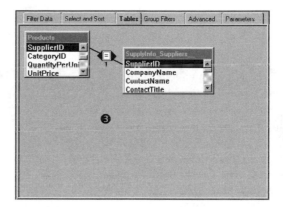

When you add a table to a query, the Query Builder looks for columns in the two tables that have the same name and type and assumes that you are joining on equal values of the joining columns. If no column name and type matches are found, a message window alerts you that you will have to manually join the tables. ■

Join the Imported_data_from_ FixWidth_txt table

In this task, you join the Imported_data_from_FixWidth_txt and Products tables. Both tables have a CategoryID column, so the join is automatic.

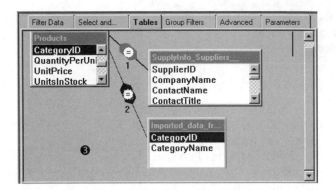

❶ In the Query Builder, click **Add Data**.

❷ In the Add Data window, click the **Project** tab and double-click the **Imported data from FixWidth.txt** data set.

❸ In the Query Builder, drag the Imported_data_from_FixWidth_txt table down so that you can see the join symbol. Click the join symbol, and notice that the files have been automatically joined on the CategoryID column.

View the data and rename the query

In this task, you view the table that was created when you joined the three individual tables. Then you rename the query item in the Project window.

❶ In the Query Builder, click **Run Query** to run the query and view the combined table.

❷ Scroll the data grid to the right, and notice the following:

- all of the columns from the three tables are included in the combined table

- there are duplicate CategoryID and SupplierID columns.

❸ Close the data grid.

❹ In the Project window, right-click the **Query1 for Products** query item and select **Rename**. Type `AllProdInfo` for the new query name.

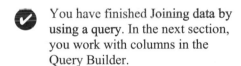

You have finished Joining data by using a query. In the next section, you work with columns in the Query Builder.

Working with columns in a query

Using the Query Builder, you can do the following:

- select the columns that you want in the query results
- specify column order and sort priorities
- change column properties, such as labels and formats
- replace values in a column
- create a new column.

In this section, you select columns so that you have only the information that you need to create your reports. You also specify sort priorities and replace the numeric values in the Discontinued column with text.

Select columns

In this task, you modify the query that you just created in order to select only the columns that you want to include in the new combined table.

❶ In the Project window, double-click **AllProdInfo**.

❷ In the Query Builder, click the **Select and Sort** tab.

❸ By default, all columns are listed for the query. Because you need only a few columns from each table, you can delete all of the selected columns and then select the columns that you want from the list on the left side of the Query Builder window. Click **Select All** and then click **Delete**.

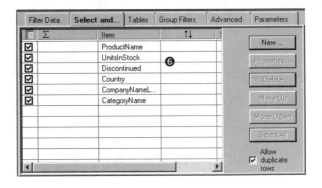

❹ From the list of columns for the Products table, double-click **ProductName**, **UnitsInStock**, and **Discontinued** to add them to the query.

❺ From the list of columns for the SupplyInfo_Suppliers table, double-click **Country** and **CompanyNameLong** to add them to the query.

❻ From the list of columns for the Imported_data_from_FixWidth_txt table, double-click **CategoryName**. The list of columns on your **Select and Sort** tab should match the one that is pictured at right.

Arrange columns in order

In this task, you arrange the columns in the order in which you want them to appear in the table.

❶ Click Country to select it. Then click Move Up until Country is the first column listed.

❷ Follow the same process until you have the columns in the following order:

Country
CategoryName
CompanyNameLong
ProductName
UnitsInStock
Discontinued.

The list of columns on your **Select and Sort** tab should match the list shown at right.

Specify sort orders

In this task, you can specify how the data is sorted in the resulting query by setting sort orders.

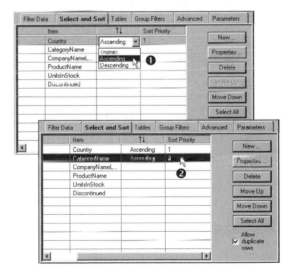

❶ On the Select and Sort tab, click inside the sort type box to the right of Country. From the drop-down list that opens, select Ascending. The sort priority is automatically set to 1.

❷ Click inside the sort type box to the right of CategoryName and select Ascending. The sort priority is set to 2.

Replace values

Using the Query Builder, you can replace the values in a column with something that you specify. In this task, you replace the numeric values in the Discontinued column with descriptive text.

❶ On the **Select and Sort** tab, click **Discontinued** to select it. Then click **Properties**.

❷ In the Properties window, click the **Replace Values** tab.

❸ Click the drop-down list below the **Replace** option. The values 1 and 0 are in the list. Select 0.

❹ In the **Replace with** box, type `Available`. Click **Add to List**.

❺ Click the drop-down list below the **Replace** option again and select 1.

❻ In the **Replace with** box, type `Discontinued`. Click **Add to List**.

❼ Click **OK**. On the **Select and Sort** tab, notice that the Discontinued column is marked with a leading underscore to show that it has been modified.

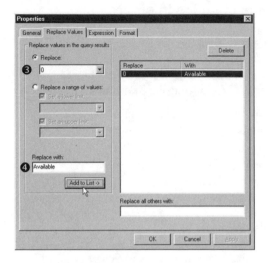

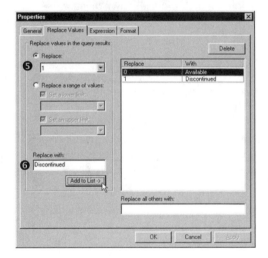

View the data

In this task, you view the results of the modified query in the data grid.

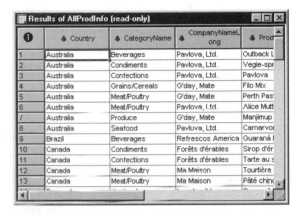

❶ Click **Run Query**. In the confirmation message, click **Yes** to overwrite the previous query results. The data opens in the data grid. Notice that the data is sorted first by Country and then by CategoryName.

❷ Scroll through the data grid to view the _Discontinued column. Notice that the data values 1 and 0 have been replaced with the text that you specified.

❸ Close the data grid.

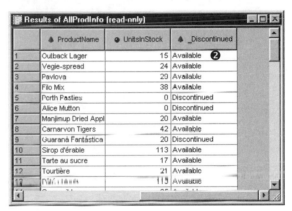

✔ You have finished Working with columns in a query. In the next section, you create a frequency count from the query data.

Creating a frequency count

Your company wants to feature the products of a different country in each of the next few catalogs that it mails. To plan the promotion, it needs to know what countries have a wide selection of products that can be featured.

In this section, you use the One-Way Frequencies task to generate a count and distribution of products from each country. In this task, you also select an option that creates a bar chart of the information. At the end of this section, you will have a report like the one below.

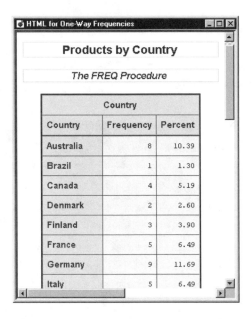

Start the task and assign variables to roles

In this task, you start the One-Way Frequencies task and then assign variables to roles.

❶   In the Project window, select the AllProdInfo query.

❷   Scroll through the Tasks by Category list to the Descriptive category. Double-click One-Way Frequencies. The task window opens.

❸   On the Columns tab, drag Country to the Analysis variables role.

Select statistics and plots

In this task, you select the statistics to perform on the Country variable. Then you select an option that creates a plot from the results of the frequency count.

❶ Click the Statistics tab.

❷ In the Frequency table options area, select the Frequencies and percentages option.

❸ Click the Plots tab.

❹ In the Bar charts area, select the Horizontal check box.

Add titles and footnotes

In this task, you add a customized title to the report and the plot and you delete the default footnote.

❶ Click the Titles tab.

❷ In the Section box, select One-Way Frequencies. In the Text box, delete both lines of text and type Products by Country.

❸ In the Section box, select Plot Titles. In the Text box, delete both lines of text and type Products by Country.

❹ In the Section box, select Footnotes. Delete the default footnote in the Text box.

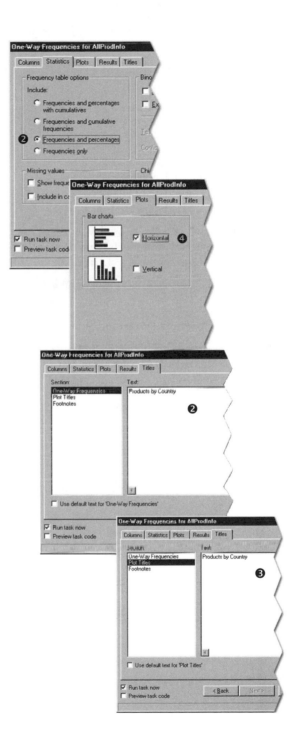

View the results

In this task, you view the results of the frequency count.

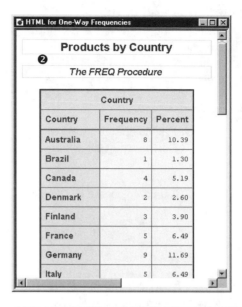

❶ In the One-Way Frequencies for AllProdInfo window, click **Finish** to create the report.

❷ Look at the report. Notice that the number of products from each country is listed in the Frequency column and the percentage of products from each country is also listed.

❸ Scroll through the results window to the plot. The number of products from each country is shown in the bar chart.

❹ Close the HTML for One-Way Frequencies window.

 You have finished **Creating a frequency count**. In the next section, you create a listing report from the query data.

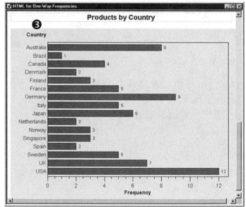

Creating a listing report from query data

You have created a report that shows the count and distribution of products by country, but you need more specific information to help plan the catalog spotlights on each country. A list of products and food categories that are arranged by country will help in this planning. This report will use information from all three tables that you joined in the query.

In this section, you use the List Data task to create a report that lists products and groups them by country. When you finish this section, you will have a report like the one below.

Start the task and assign variables to roles

In this task, you start the List Data task and assign variables to roles.

❶ In the Project window, select **AllProdInfo** to make it active.

❷ Scroll through the **Tasks by Category** list to the Descriptive category. Double-click List Data. The task window opens.

❸ On the **Columns** tab, drag **ProductName** and **CategoryName** to the **List variables** role.

❹ Drag **Country** to the **Group table by** role and again to the **Identifying label** role.

Add column labels

In this task, you add labels to columns. The labels are used as column headings in the results.

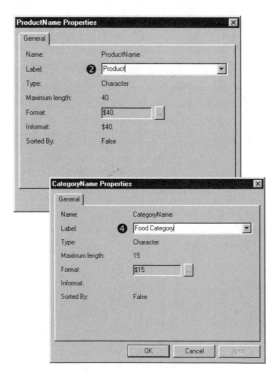

❶ On the **Columns** tab of the List Data for AllProdInfo window, right-click **ProductName** and select **Properties**. The ProductName Properties window opens.

❷ In the **Label** box, delete the existing text and type `Product`. Click **OK**.

❸ On the **Columns** tab of the List Data for AllProdInfo window, right-click **CategoryName** and select **Properties**. The CategoryName Properties window opens.

❹ In the **Label** box, delete the existing text and type `Food Category`. Click **OK**.

Set options and specify a title

In this task, you set options and specify a title for
the report.

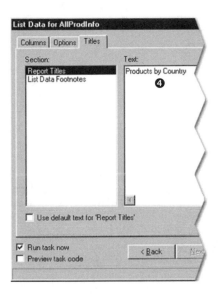

❶ Click the Options tab.

❷ Clear the Print the row number check box.

❸ Click the Titles tab. In the Section box,
select Report Titles.

❹ In the Text box, delete the default title and
type Products by Country.

❺ In the Section box, select List Data
Footnotes. In the Text box, delete the default
footnote.

View the results

In this task, you view the results of the List
Data task.

❶ Click Finish. The results of the List Data
task open automatically.

❷ Scroll through the results. Notice that the
products are grouped by country. The labels
that you specified for ProductName and
CategoryName are used in the results.

❸ Close the HTML for List Data window.

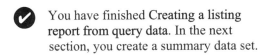
✓ You have finished Creating a listing
report from query data. In the next
section, you create a summary data set.

Chapter 7

Summarizing Data and Creating Reports

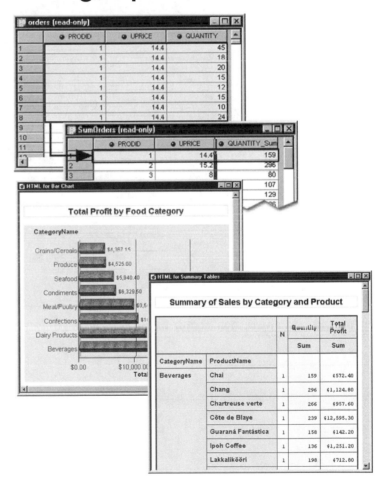

Creating summary data

The Summary Statistics task provides data summarization tools to compute descriptive statistics for variables across all observations and within groups of observations.

The next two reports that you create focus on product sales and profit data for each food category. The company is interested in which food categories generate the most profit and sales. To create these reports, you need sales data along with the data that you already have in the AllProdInfo query. The Orders table has data on sales, but it has numerous entries for each product identification number. The data must be summarized before it is added to the AllProdInfo query.

In this section, you use the Summary Statistics task to create a SAS table that summarizes QUANTITY by PRODID, as shown below.

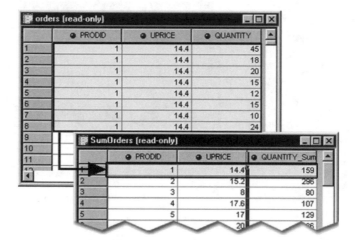

Open and view the Orders data

In this task, you open the Orders table and sort the data.

❶ In the Project window, double-click the Orders icon. The table opens in the data grid.

❷ By default, tables are opened in read-only mode. To sort data, you must unprotect the data. From the menu bar, select **Data ➔ Protected**. In the confirmation box, click **Yes**.

❸ Right-click the PRODID column and select **Sort ➔ Ascending**. Notice that there are multiple entries for each PRODID. To get the total quantity that has been ordered for each PRODID, you can use the Summary Statistics task.

❹ Select **Data ➔ Protected** to re-protect the data, and then close the Orders data grid.

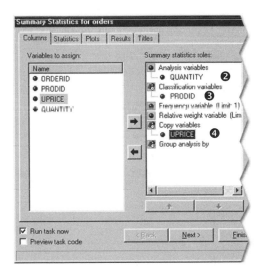

Start the task and assign variables to roles

In this task, you start the Summary Statistics task and assign variables to roles.

❶ Scroll through the Tasks by Category list to the Descriptive category. Double-click Summary Statistics. The task window opens.

❷ On the Columns tab, drag QUANTITY to the Analysis variables role.

❸ Drag PRODID to the Classification variables role.

❹ Drag UPRICE to the Copy variables role. This copies the UPRICE variable into the output data set.

Select statistics

In this task, you select the statistic to perform on the variable that is being analyzed.

❶ Click the Statistics tab. Click Deselect All to clear the default statistics selections.

❷ Select the Sum check box.

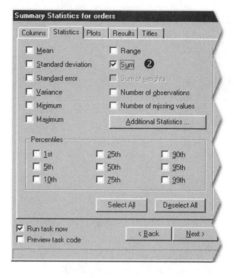

Generate the output data set

In this task, you generate the summary data.

❶ Click the Results tab.

❷ Select the Save statistics to output data table check box and leave the default location selected.

❸ Clear the Show statistics check box.

❹ Click Finish. The output data opens in the data grid and is added to the project. Close the data grid.

✔ You have finished Creating summary data. The next task is to add the data to the AllProdInfo query.

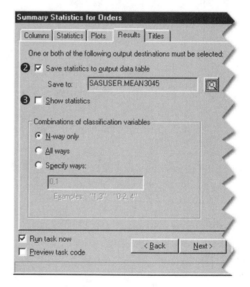

Adding data to an existing query

In this section you add the summary data to the AllProdInfo query. The values in the PRODID column in the Summary_statistics_for_Orders table correspond to the values in the ProductID column in the Products table. Because the columns have different names, you must specify which columns you want to join. After the summary data is added, the query will have sales data for each product.

In this section, you add data to the query and create a computed column for total profit. With sales and profit information available for each product, you can create a bar chart of total profit by food category, and a summary table of sales by category and product.

Manually join the new table

In this task, you add a third table to the AllProdInfo query. The column names for the product ID columns differ in the two tables, so you must join the tables manually.

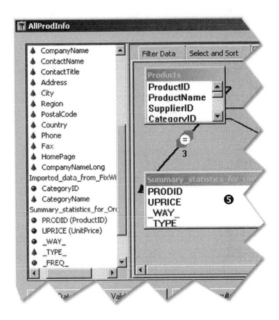

❶ In the Project window, double-click AllProdInfo to open the query.

❷ In the AllProdInfo query window, click **Add Data**.

❸ In the Add Data window, click the **Project** tab. Double-click **Summary statistics for Orders**. A message window opens to inform you to join the tables manually. Click **OK**.

❹ On the **Tables** tab, drag the Summary_statistics_for_Orders table below the Products table.

❺ To manually join the tables, you must specify which columns in each table should be joined. Select **ProductID** in the Products list and drag the mouse pointer to PRODID in the Summary_statistics_for_Orders table. The two tables are joined.

Select columns and change column properties

In this task, you delete some unnecessary columns from the Summary_statistics_for_Orders table. You also create an alias for one of the remaining columns.

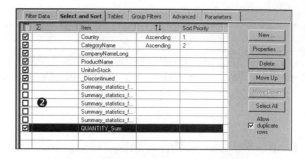

❶ In the AllProdInfo query window, click the **Select and Sort** tab.

❷ Clear the check boxes next to PRODID, UPRICE, _WAY_ , _TYPE_, and _FREQ_.

❸ Select the QUANTITY_Sum column, then click **Properties**.

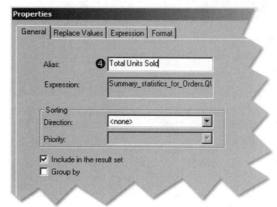

❹ In the **Alias** box, type `Total Units Sold`.

❺ Click **OK**. The QUANTITY_Sum column is renamed in the list on the **Select and Sort** tab.

Create a computed column

You can use the Query Builder to create a computed column. Because the column is created in the query instead of in the data grid, the values will be updated if the underlying data changes. In this task you create a column for total profit.

❶ On the Select and Sort tab of the AllProdInfo query window, click **New**.

❷ In the **Alias** box, type `Total Profit`.

❸ Click the **Expression** tab. Notice that at the top of the tab, there is a white box for the expression that will be used to create the new column. You can either type an expression in this box or construct an expression by using the operator buttons and the **Functions** and **Values** tabs.

❹ Click the **Values** tab below the row of operator buttons.

❺ In the **Data Source** box, be sure that Products is selected. In the **Value** box, double-click UnitPrice.

❻ Click the subtraction operator.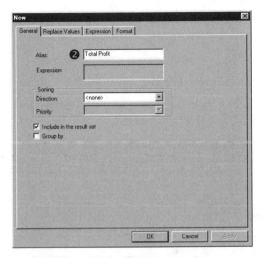

❼ In the **Data Source** box, select Summary_statistics_for_Orders In the **Value** box, double-click UPRICE.

❽ Highlight the expression that you have created so far, and click the parentheses operator.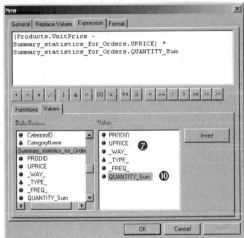

The parentheses should enclose the expression as follows:
```
(Products.UnitPrice -
Summary_statistics_for_Orders
.UPRICE)
```

❾ Click the multiplication operator.

❿ In the **Value** box, double-click QUANTITY_Sum.

Adding data to an existing query

Add a format to the new column

In this task, you specify a format for the values of the computed column.

❶ In the New window, click the **Format** tab.

❷ In the **Categories** box, select **Currency**.

❸ In the **Formats** box, select **DOLLARw.d**.

❹ In the **Attributes** area, change **Overall width** to 10 and **Decimal places** to 2.

❺ Click **OK** to close the New window.

Export the data to Microsoft Excel

In this task, you export the results of the query to a Microsoft Excel file.

❶ In the AllProdInfo query window, click **Run Query** to update the query. In the confirmation window, click **Yes** to overwrite the previous results. The data opens in the data grid.

❷ In the Project window, right-click **Results of AllProdInfo** and select **Save Results of AllProdInfo As/Export**. In the Save As window, click the Personal folder icon and choose a location for the file.

❸ From the **Save as type** list, select **Microsoft Excel Files(*.xls)**. You can accept the default name or enter a different name.

❹ Click **Save**.

❺ Close the Results of AllProdInfo data grid.

✔ You have finished **Adding data to an existing query**. The next task is to create a bar chart from the query.

Creating a bar chart from query data

In this section, you use the Bar Chart task to generate a bar chart that shows total profit for each food category. You also customize the appearance of the chart. When you finish this section, you will have a chart like the one below.

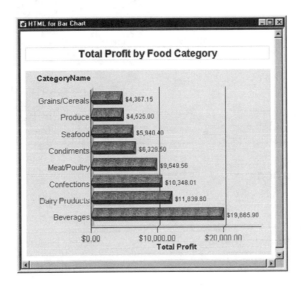

Start the task and select a chart type

In this task, you start the Bar Chart task and select a horizontal bar chart.

❶ In the Project window, select the AllProdInfo query to make it the active data.

❷ Scroll through the Tasks by Category list to the Graph category. Double-click **Bar**. The task window opens.

❸ On the **Chart Gallery** tab, double-click the Simple Horizontal Bar icon.

Assign variables to roles

In this task, you first select a column to chart and then a sum column that determines the lengths of the bars.

❶ On the **Columns** tab, drag CategoryName to the **Column to chart** role.

❷ Drag Total Profit to the **Sum by** role.

Customize the appearance

You can customize the appearance of your graph by setting the options that are available on the **Appearance** tab. In this task, you change the color and shape of the bars and add a title to the bar chart.

❶ Click the **Appearance** tab. Notice the buttons across the top of the tab for customizing various aspects of the chart. The **Bars** button is selected the first time you open this tab.

❷ Click the **Textures** tab below the button bar. Browse the textures and select one that you like.

❸ Click the **Layout** button.

❹ From the **Shape** drop-down list, select **Prism**.

❺ From the **Order** drop-down list, select **Ascending**.

❻ Click the **Titles** button. In the **Title** box, type `Total Profit by Food Category`.

❼ Delete the text in the **Footnote** box.

Create the chart

In this task, you generate and view the bar chart.

❶ In the Bar Chart for AllProdInfo window, click Finish to create the bar chart.

❷ Look at the bar chart. The chart shows the total profit that was generated by products in each food category.

❸ Close the HTML for Bar Chart window.

 You have finished Creating a bar chart from query data. In the next section, you create a summary table with sales and profit information.

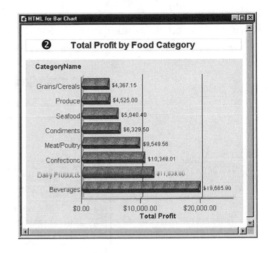

Creating a summary table

Using the Summary Tables task, you can display descriptive statistics in tabular format for some or all of the columns in a table.

In this section, you create a summary table that displays sales and profit information by category and product. When you finish this section, you will have a report that looks like the one below.

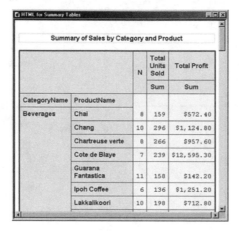

Start the task and assign variables to roles

In this task, you start the Summary Tables task and assign variables to roles.

❶ In the Project window, select the AllProdInfo query.

❷ Scroll through the Tasks by Category list to the Descriptive category. Double-click Summary Tables. The task window opens.

❸ On the Columns tab, drag Total Units Sold and Total Profit to the Analysis variables role.

❹ Drag CategoryName and ProductName to the Classification variables role.

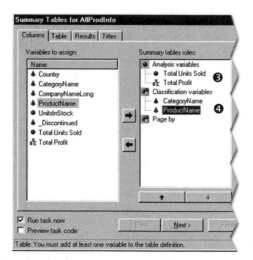

Design the table

When you create a summary table, you need to decide how you want the classification and analysis variables to appear in the table. In this task, you display the classification variables as rows and the analysis variables as columns.

❶ Click the Table tab.

❷ Drag ProductName into the white box on the left side of the Preview area so that it is displayed as a row in the table.

❸ Drag CategoryName to the left of the ProductName variable so that the ProductName rows are grouped by CategoryName. When you are positioning the CategoryName variable to the left of ProductName, the border turns blue when the mouse pointer is in the correct position, and an arrow appears that indicates where the variable will be positioned.

❹ Drag Total Units Sold to the right of the N column in the top portion of the Preview area so that it is displayed as a column in the table.

❺ Drag Total Profit to the right of the Total Units Sold variable.

📋 You might need to scroll the column area to the right before you can drop the Total Profit variable to the right of the Total Units Sold variable. ∎

ⓘ To maximize the task window and increase the size of the Preview area, click the Expand to fill the desktop tool ☐ at the top right of the Preview area.

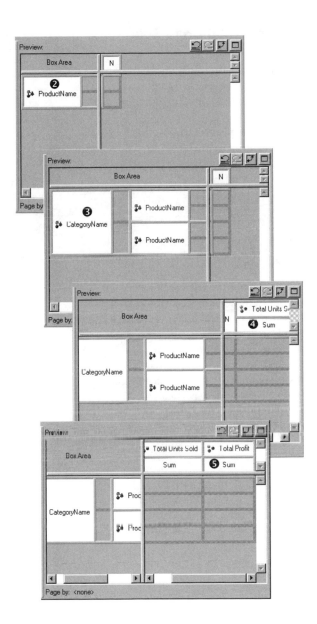

Format the Total Units Sold column

In this task, you format the data in the Total Units Sold column so that it is displayed with no decimal places.

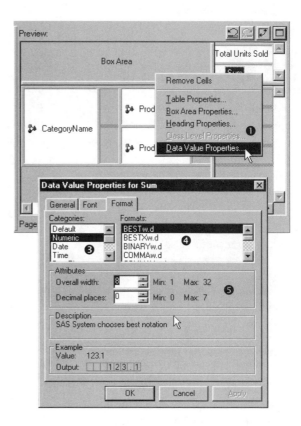

❶ In the **Preview** area, right-click the Sum heading below the Total Units Sold column heading and select **Data Value Properties**.

❷ In the Data Value Properties for Sum window, click the **Format** tab.

❸ In the **Categories** list, select **Numeric**.

❹ In the **Formats** list, select **BESTw.d**.

❺ In the **Attributes** area, set **Overall width** to 8. Leave **Decimal places** set to 0.

❻ Click **OK**.

❼ In the **Preview** area, right-click the Total Units Sold column heading and select **Heading Properties**.

❽ In the **Label** box, delete the text and type `Total Units Sold`. Click OK.

Format the Total Profit column

In this task, you format the data in the Total Profit column so that it appears with a dollar sign and two decimal places.

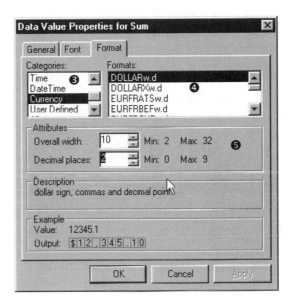

❶ In the Preview area, right-click the Sum heading below the Total Profit column heading and select Data Value Properties.

❷ In the Data Value Properties for Sum window, click the Format tab.

❸ In the Categories list, select Currency.

❹ In the Formats list, select DOLLARw.d.

❺ In the Attributes area, set Overall width to 10 and Decimal places to 2.

❻ Click OK.

Add titles and footnotes

In this task, you add a customized title to the report, and you delete the footnote.

❶ Click the Titles tab.

❷ In the Section box, select Table Titles. The default title is Summary Tables Results.

❸ In the Text box, delete the default title and type Summary of Sales by Category and Product.

❹ In the Section box, select Footnotes. In the Text box, delete the default footnote.

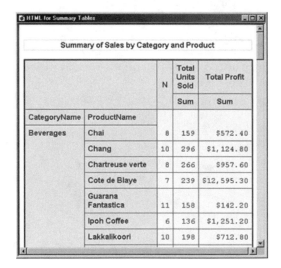

View the results

In this task, you view the results of the Summary Table task.

❶ In the Summary Tables for AllProdInfo window, click Finish to create the report.

❷ Scroll through the results. Notice that products are grouped by category and that Quantity and Total Profit are listed for each product, as you specified when you designed the table. Also, notice that the data values in the Quantity and Total Profit columns have the formats that you applied.

❸ Close the HTML for Summary Tables window.

✔ You have finished **Creating a summary table**. Congratulations! You have completed the book. The next page lists some additional resources for learning about SAS software.

Index

E

EG Default style, 34, 35
Expand to fill desktop tool, 73
exporting query results to Microsoft Excel, 68
Expression tab, 67
external browser, 29

F

field options, 20
field widths, 20
filtered data
    creating listing reports from, 41–43
filtering data, 38–40
fixed-width text files, 19
footnotes
    for frequency counts, 55
    for summary tables, 76
format of data, 16
format of output, 36
formats for column data, 68, 74, 75
frequency counts, 54–56
    assigning variables, 54
    footnotes, 55
    statistics and plots, 55
    titles, 55
    viewing results, 56

G

graph controls, 32
graph types, 33
graphics options, 32
graphs. *See also* bar charts
    customizing appearance, 70
    pie charts, 33
    saving, 33

H

headings for columns, 58
help, 10
horizontal bar charts, 69

I

Import Data task, 19–21
importing data from text files, 19–21

J

joining data
    manually joining tables, 65
    with queries, 46–49

L

labels
    bar chart columns, 31
    listing report columns, 58
List Data task
    listing reports, 24–29
    listing reports from filtered data, 41–43
    listing reports from query data, 57–59
listing reports
    assigning variables, 25, 42, 58
    column labels, 58
    creating, 24–29
    from filtered data, 41–43
    from query data, 57–59
    modifying, 28–29
    saving without running, 27
    selecting data, 24
    setting options, 26, 43, 59
    titles, 43, 59
    viewing results, 27, 29, 43, 59

M

manually joining tables, 65
maximizing windows, 73
Microsoft Excel files
    adding data to projects, 18
    creating data sets from, 19–21
    exporting query results to, 68

N

notes for projects, 14

O

One-Way Frequencies task, 54–56
opening projects, 6
opening SAS Enterprise Guide, 6
options
    data options for bar charts, 32
    field options, 20
    graphics options, 32
    setting for listing reports, 26, 43, 59
Options tab, 26
ordering
    columns, 51
    project items, 17
    variables, 25
output data sets, 64
output formats, 36

P

pie charts, 33
plots, 55
Preview area
    increasing, 73
previewing task code, 26
Products table, 24
project files, 15

Project window, 8

deleting items from, 18
restoring, 8
projects
    adding data sets to, 17
    adding data to, 16–18
    adding Microsoft Excel files to, 18
    creating, 6
    notes for, 14
    opening, 6
    order of items in, 17
    saving, 15
    setting up, 14–15
properties
    bar properties, 32
    column properties, 66
    table properties, 21
    variable properties, 25

Q

queries
    adding summary data to, 65–68
    adding tables to, 47
    columns in, 50–53
    creating bar charts from data, 69–71
    creating listing reports from data, 57–59
    exporting results to Microsoft Excel, 68
    joining data, 46–49
    renaming, 49
    running tasks against, 42
    viewing data, 49
Query Builder
    adding tables to queries, 47
    columns in queries, 50–53
    creating computed columns, 67
    filtering data, 38–40
    joining data, 46–49
    starting, 38

R

renaming
    imported files, 21
    queries, 49
replacing column values, 52
report styles
    applying, 36
    creating, 35
    customizing, 34–36
    saving, 35
reports. *See* listing reports
restoring Project window, 8
running tasks against queries, 42

S

SAS code
    viewing, 26
SAS Display Manager System (DMS), 3
SAS Enterprise Guide
    customizing, 7
    data in, 16
    description of, 2
    opening, 6
    touring, 7–10
SAS formats for column data, 68, 74, 75
SAS Learning Edition, 2–3
SAS programming, 3
saving
    graphs, 33
    listing reports, without running, 27
    projects, 15
    report styles, 35
.seg file extension, 15
selecting
    chart type, 30, 69
    columns, 50, 66
    data for listing reports, 24
    statistics for summary data, 64
setting up projects, 14–15
sort order for column data, 51

SQL code
    viewing, 38
statistics
    for frequency counts, 55
    for summary data, 64
    Summary Statistics task, 62–64
styles. *See* report styles
summary data, 62–68
    adding to queries, 65–68
    assigning variables, 63
    creating, 62–64
    output data set, 64
    selecting statistics, 64
Summary Statistics task, 62–64
summary tables
    analysis variables in, 73
    assigning variables, 72
    classification variables in, 73
    creating, 72–76
    designing, 73
    footnotes, 76
    formatting column data, 74, 75
    titles, 76
    viewing results, 76
Summary Tables task, 72–76

T

table format for data, 16
tables
    designing summary tables, 73
    joining data, 46–49
    manually joining, 65
    properties, 21
Task List, 9

Learning More

Try it on your own

If you have worked through all of the tasks in this book, you have learned to use many of the features of SAS Enterprise Guide and are ready to work with your own data. As you try new tasks and features, don't forget to use the Enterprise Guide Help if you need more information.

Explore more resources for learning

The SAS Learning Edition community (support.sas.com/le) was created to help you get the most from SAS Learning Edition. Depending on what you want to learn, you will find links to resources such as SAS Self-Paced e-Learning courses, classroom training, and books. The Web site also has links to the General and Technical Q&A pages for SAS Learning Edition.

e-Learning

The SAS Self-Paced e-Learning catalog (support.sas.com/selfpaced) provides you with immediate access to over 60 lessons and courses that teach you how to perform various tasks by using SAS Learning Edition. The tasks range from using SAS programming to access, manage, analyze, and present data to performing queries, creating reports, and performing statistical analyses by using the SAS Enterprise Guide interface. You can also prepare for the SAS basic programmer and advanced programmer certification exams with courses that are designed for this purpose.

Instructor-based training

The list of SAS Enterprise Guide training courses (http://support.sas.com/training/us/prod_eg.html) includes both classroom and live Web courses on topics such as querying and reporting, statistical analyses, and customizing results.

SAS Learning Edition Q & A

Q. What are the limitations of SAS Learning Edition?
A. SAS Learning Edition works with data sets of any size, but it processes and displays only the first 1000 observations (rows) in your data set. SAS Learning Edition does, however, handle an unlimited number of variables (columns). Also, the SAS procedures that are included with SAS Learning Edition are those that are surfaced by SAS Enterprise Guide. For a complete list of SAS procedures that are included with this product, please visit support.sas.com/le.

Q. What support is included?
A. Limited product support is available via the SAS Learning Edition Web site (support.sas.com/le). Here you will find links under General Resources for General Q & A, Technical Q & A, SAS Notes, and Installation information. You can also use the Contact Us link at the top right of the Web page to ask any questions that you may have.

Q. Where is the sample data and sample code located for SAS Learning Edition?
A. If you accepted the defaults when you installed SAS Learning Edition, the sample data is located in

```
C:\Program Files\SAS\EG Learning Edition 2.0\Sample\Data
```

and the sample code is located in

```
C:\Program Files\SAS\EG Learning Edition 2.0\Sample\Code.
```

Q. How do I import and export data with SAS Learning Edition?
A. To import data, use the Import Data task in SAS Enterprise Guide. You can open the task by selecting Tools ➜ Import Data from the main menu. You can use this tool to import text files and Microsoft Excel files. To export data, select File ➜ Save As/Export.

Q. Can I specify data library locations in SAS Learning Edition?
A. Yes. To assign a library you must issue a LIBNAME statement in the Code Editor window

Q. Can I write my own macros with SAS Learning Edition?
A. Yes. This product has full macro programming capabilities. You can write your own SAS macros by using the Code Editor window. To access the Code Editor window, select Insert ➜ Code. Note, however, that the autocall library of pre-written macros is not included with SAS Learning Edition.

Q. Can I use SAS Learning Edition to learn SAS programming?
A. Yes. Although the Getting Started tutorial and book focus on the point-and-click features of SAS Enterprise Guide, you can use SAS Enterprise Guide to write, edit, and submit SAS programs. SAS Learning Edition has a code window where you can either import existing SAS code (sample code is provided with the product) and modify it, or write your own SAS programs in the easy-to-use, color-coded, syntax-checking code window. To access the Code Editor window, select **Code** from the **Insert** menu and choose either the **New** or **Existing** tab, depending on whether you want to write your own code or modify existing code. In addition, you can read databases and perform data manipulation. Please keep in mind, however, that this product is for self-training, non-production use only. In addition, SAS Self-Paced e-Learning has numerous courses and lessons that you can take using SAS Learning Edition, including an entire SAS programming course. For more information, visit `support.sas.com/selfpaced`.

Q. What if I really want to use the SAS windowing environment (SAS Explorer, Enhanced Editor, Log, and Output windows) instead of SAS Enterprise Guide?
A. If you are a SAS user who prefers to use the SAS windowing environment, you can add a shortcut to your desktop that will start SAS rather than SAS Enterprise Guide. Just follow these instructions:

❶ On your desktop, right-click **My Computer** and select **Explore** from the pop-up menu.

❷ Navigate to the directory where you installed SAS Learning Edition.

❸ Right-click sas.exe and select **Copy**.

❹ On your desktop, right-click and select **Paste shortcut**.

❺ A SAS V8 icon now appears on your desktop.

IMPORTANT NOTE: SAS/AF run-time support is not included in SAS Learning Edition. As a result, you cannot use the following tools in the SAS windowing environment:

Import Wizard
Export Wizard
VIEWTABLE.

If you try to open one of these tools, you will receive an error message in the log.